T0131637

THE INDIGO SOUL

a child's journey to purpose

2ND EDITION

ARNETTE LAMOREAUX

BALBOA.
PRESS
A DIVISION OF HAY HOUSE

Author Credits
INDIGO SCOUT: come closer, your purpose is calling

Book cover design by Natalie J Stott
Indigo healing hands:
Jonah R. - 5 months
Gracelynne S. - 3 years
Jacob L. - 18 years

Images provided by:
Andy Sharp
Arnette Lamoreaux
Erynn Lamoreaux
Eileen Poldermans
Maris Michael George

Balboa Press books may be ordered through booksellers or by contacting:

Balboa Press
A Division of Hay House
1663 Liberty Drive
Bloomington, IN 47403
www.balboapress.com
1 (877) 407-4847

Print information available on the last page.

ISBN: 978-1-5043-4236-0 (sc)
ISBN: 978-1-5043-4237-7 (e)

Library of Congress Control Number: 2015917604

Balboa Press rev. date: 12/9/2015

I lovingly dedicate this book to
My wondrous Indigo Souls
Jacob and Erynn.

To each Indigo Aware resource, with their unique skill set,
Who amazingly arrived exactly when I needed them.

To the Indigo Scouts who finally made it to our door.

And to all the Navigators with Indigo Souls in their care,
Who will find our door
Wide open.

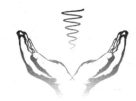

CONTENTS

FOREWORD

By Dan Viotto, Indigo Aware

The first time I heard the term "Indigo" was maybe three years ago. To be quite honest, I didn't give it much thought. My friend, Arnette, had visited with a spiritual healer and had learned that both of her kids were Indigo. In my world, where my wife and I do not have children, it seemed a bit kooky and new age and since it was not something that I had to personally deal with on a regular basis, it was pretty much a situation of "out of sight out of mind."

By training I am a business man. For over 20 years I have been involved in business-to-business sales in the electronics, construction, healthcare, and media industries. I have consulted companies on how to become more efficient and help them to improve their revenue by aligning their sales and marketing teams. Recently, I was asked to join a small marketing and branding company to help them prepare to grow and to expose them to larger enterprise level clients.

Do I fit the mold of someone that should be writing the forward to a book about Indigo Souls? At first glance absolutely not. However, over the past few years, people, events, and what at the time seemed like complete coincidences have presented themselves to me that have led me to an awakening that I could not fathom just a few short years ago. I have become conscious of concepts and tools to help me deal with life in a more connected way. I want to make sure that I don't confuse this with a religious awakening in the traditional sense. I have respect for religion, all religion, but I do not feel that one religion is any more important or relevant than any other. What has happened to me personally has led me to believe that all energy, be it people, or animals, or the environment are connected in a vast oneness. I know, that does sound pretty kooky and new age for a traditional guy, right?

I've been leading what you could call an ordinary life; concerned mainly with the ups and downs of balancing a stressful work life and trying to figure out how to have an even better home life with my wife. Living in Austin, there are ample opportunities to expose oneself to any number of "non-western" healing modalities. My first exposure to anything other than a standard doctor visit was with a Doctor of Oriental Medicine, an acupuncturist. My brother-in-law who is a highly respected businessman and who prior to his retirement, was a division president for a very well known multi-billion dollar company told me how he was able to get back to playing pain free golf after a few visits. I had recently had a rather embarrassing fall out of a hammock (it's okay for you to laugh at this point), and had basically cracked my tailbone. I decided to give it a try. This holistic healer was able to immediately relieve the pain by restoring natural energy flow through the area. Had I seen a "regular" doctor, I am sure I would have been sent home with a painkiller and little more. Even more interesting to me than the benefit received from acupuncture was the talk about the Angels that were there with me in the room. Okay, now we were really getting into that weird hippy area. She also was quite aware and well-versed on what it meant to be Indigo. This meeting proved to be a pivotal point in my life and much learning has taken place since that time. Again, you have to realize that this was completely new and different from the standard learning I had received in school and business.

Modern physics talks about string theory and posits that at its most sub-atomic level, everything in the universe is made up of vibrating strings and that these strings vibrate in 11 dimensions. At its core, everything vibrates to its own frequency. If that is the case, then it is safe to assume that human beings vibrate as well; each at a different frequency, but vibrating nonetheless. This book will give the reader a much better understanding of what "being Indigo" means. Part of what makes these souls unique is that they are capable of vibrating at a higher frequency. This higher frequency allows them to do remarkable things in terms of healing.

Many of you who have found this book, or have had it given to you by a friend or counselor, are likely facing the challenges of raising an Indigo Soul and are struggling with how to get your child to be successful in a traditional education system. Clearly, our system is not prepared or designed to handle "one-offs" and anyone that does not fit is, more often than not, left behind. I have heard it said that if Albert Einstein were to take part in the current educational system in our country, he would have been tagged with a label, possibly ADD or ADHD, and not allowed to flourish because he was "different." He is arguably one of the most brilliant thinkers of the modern era and he likely would not have succeeded by today's standards. Who is to say that every human soul needs to be educated by rules that were established in a different time and era? Test scores in all areas are plummeting in the United States in comparison to other countries and parents, politicians, and educators are trying to find new ways to provide education that resonates with our children and prepares them for a world that is rapidly changing. For those Indigo Souls who are struggling to survive or worse yet, have given up on trying, a different way of thinking is a necessity. I am not saying that every child that struggles in school is Indigo but those that are, indeed Indigo, need to be put on a new path which will benefit the world in ways that we cannot yet comprehend. I have had a shift in consciousness. I invite you to open your mind to new possibilities and perhaps find some answers to questions you may be struggling to answer.

PREFACE

My style of writing is probably not what you would expect. Could it have been more formal? Absolutely. But to know me is to understand that most things about me are relatively relaxed: casual house, casual clothes, casual parenting and now, casual writing. My thought process may seem random though I prefer to think of it as "efficient." My goal is to not be too clinical, nor to bare a mess of emotions. I consider it fortunate, but some may not, that I am able to compartmentalize my feelings. Though this experience was overwhelming to say the least, I had to maintain some semblance of normality in front of my kids. I have always followed the adage that if I don't make a big production, then they won't make a big production. It has worked well for me so far.

I also want to note that I do believe traditional education is sufficient for many of the children out there; it was sufficient for me! Unfortunately, we as a society have not demanded that our educational system be "overhauled." We currently only accommodate a child if something is quantifiably "different."

Albert Einstein said "Everybody is a genius. But if you judge a fish by its ability to climb a tree, it will live its whole life believing that it is stupid." A very talented artist drew this illustration for me.

"For a fair selection everybody has to take the same exam: Please climb that tree."

Our kids may look the same on the outside, but their learning styles (even if not medically diagnosed) can be as different as an elephant in comparison to a penguin! Little did I know that was just the tip of the iceburg.

This book is a team effort between me and Abraham. If you are not yet familiar with Abraham: Abraham is a group consciousness of high vibrational spiritual beings; beings that work through God. Their purpose is to bring humanity the wisdom and guidance of God for the advancement of our soul's journey. Though most of their work is done through human channels, Abraham does not function with ego (a human characteristic).

They have chose multiple people to work through in delivering their message; their most well known channel is Esther (and Jerry) Hicks. She has been conveying their messages and writing books with them for over 30 years. They also work with my own mentor Linda Drake[1]. It was through Linda that I was first introduced to Abraham.

And lastly, some of what you are about to read are chronicled events that have led me to where I am today. I am in no way shape or form a subject matter expert on anything Indigo. Therefore, I reference the work of other authors that have done extensive research on who and what Indigo means in western culture. I believe it would be a disservice to alter the timeline to imply I knew more than I did at any earlier point in time. Where I am now, I am able to say with conviction, that yes, my purpose is **all that is Indigo**. I continue to learn more every day.

Both my kids are different. Is yours?

~Arnette

---

[1]   Life Path Healer/Intuitive Life Coach –
       http://lindadrakeconsulting.com

GETTING STARTED
(Words from Abraham)

We have chosen you, Arnette, to hear our word, to be our voice to benefit humanity. You volunteered for this long ago knowing it will require tenacity and an overwhelming sense of right and wrong. Yet right and wrong is not always black and white. "Right" is what is best for a soul. "Wrong" is what is harmful to a soul. If mankind's rules and regulations do not have the best interest of the soul then is it your job as the guardian of this soul to determine "its" right and wrong, which is (and will always be), very different from the right and wrong of mankind *as you know it.* You have been blessed by Source as you understand through actual experiences what it means to be the guardian of an Indigo.

This is a covenant, between Arnette Lillen Lamoreaux and we that are Abraham to bring forth the voice of Source. To guide, guard, and protect the soul of the Indigo. To navigate paths, journey together, and find purpose here on Earth. You, Arnette, will lovingly guide those souls we bring you. To embrace the uniqueness that is theirs and theirs alone, and bring forth the healing that is so desperately needed at this time.

We that are Abraham are a collective being that work through Earth Angels. We lovingly embrace the uniqueness of each and every soul sent to Earth. It is now our mission to educate you the people on what is needed. To those that have embraced and committed to raising an Indigo Soul, it is important that you are made aware earlier in their human lifetime the fact that they are, that which is Indigo. Every guardian of an Indigo Soul agreed to this purpose long ago, just like Arnette. She actively challenged her own right and wrong and attempted to apply logic to that which is illogical. It has brought us to where we are today. Her ability to interpret our words, express our thoughts, in a manner for all to hear. With this, we provide you with the tools you will need as the guardian of the Indigo Soul. A child's journey to their purpose is now in your hands. And with that, we begin.

~Abraham

MEET ARNETTE

(as spoken by Abraham)

My name is Arnette Lamoreaux and I am the mother of two Indigo Children. I did not know either was Indigo until my oldest child was 15 years old. It had been heart breaking for me to watch this brilliant child wither before my eyes. He seemed broken. He felt broken, and I could not fix him. For years I reached out to others for guidance and eventually found my way to Linda Drake and Abraham. Their words provided the comfort and solace from which my own purpose was recognized. Slowly, but surely, I have learned what I must do. I am eternally grateful to those that have helped me along the way. For now I, along with Abraham, am here to help all of you. To bring you the comfort you so desperately need, and to know that you are not alone. These children are our lifeline. These children must understand their role in the greater plan sooner rather than later. Mankind cannot wait years upon years for these children to realize why they are here. They must heal. They must begin to heal that which is broken; the planet, the animals, but most of all, each other. They are here to heal all souls.

~Abraham

ARNETTE'S WORDS

MAY 2011

My son started college today. I assume that most parents are happy for this day, I certainly am. It has been a long road for my boy and also for me. Never did I imagine that his academic journey would be anything other than "the norm." Yes, some are blessed "book smart" and easily make good grades. Others may have to put forth some kind of effort needing to study a little more just to make average grades. Regardless of the effort, school is what it is. (American) society dictates that we are supposed to complete 12th grade before we are free to choose our own path. Unfortunately, some never make it through. This boy was held back a grade. This boy supplemented with Sylvan Learning Center®. This boy had private tutors. This boy was tested for learning disabilities. So much time and energy trying to understand **what** is wrong and **why** does he struggle so much. It is not supposed to be this hard! It took me awhile, but I figured out my kids Plan B. It's 1 ½ years before he is "officially" scheduled to graduate from high school. However, my son started college *today.*

JULY 1994

He's normal. Born just under 10 pounds, 20" long. He has all of his fingers and toes. I love him. Everybody loves him. Who doesn't love a baby? Over the 90th percentile for height and weight, "he's going to be a big boy" the pediatrician would say. I worked full time, but luckily grandma was daycare. He was an easy baby and an easy toddler (though very stubborn). He slept well, ate well, laughed and played. Time goes by so fast.

1998-2000

Preschool: where three to four year olds attend a local elementary school for a few hours a day. Seemed like a good idea: meet other kids, learn new things, give grandma a break. It is the precursor to starting "real" school. I remember his first day clearly. He was dressed in a matching blue sweatshirt and sweatpants, sneakers, sporting a military crew cut that was grandma's specialty (having four boys of her own). We were running a little bit late so we are the last to arrive. Walking and holding hands (we always held hands) we came through the door. The teacher approached us. I looked past her and could see the customary "circle time." The kids sit "criss-cross applesauce" (i.e. Indian style) in a circle on the floor trying to be still.

His eyes were huge, but he didn't seem scared. No tears, not clingy. I released his hand, crouched down, kissed the top of his head and said that grandma would pick him up. I figured that a quick exit strategy was the best; let the teacher handle any meltdown if one came. I could hear her whisper to him as I walked out the door. But, I didn't leave. I watched through a side window. The teacher put her arm around his shoulder to guide him to the circle. It seemed in slow motion. He ducked, turned, and spun out of her grasp. He walked toward the wall putting his back up against it and slid down to a sitting position. "Jacob" she said, "What are you doing? Come join the circle." He looked directly in her eyes and said quite clearly "I'm in a time out." She smiled and chuckled, "But Jake, you didn't do anything wrong." This time, a little bit louder and more precise he said, "I said...I'm in a timeout." She had been dismissed. She knew it. She went back and joined the circle (without him). Jake sat there and observed, and I observed him observing.

With his unblinking eyes wide open I could see the wheels turning in his head. The conversation his little three year old brain must have been having with himself probably went like this "*Why do they want me to sit on the floor in a circle with a bunch of kids I don't know? Is this supposed to be fun? Blech, that boy in the orange is picking his nose. Oh my gosh, the other boy looks like he's about to explode, he cannot sit still. Well, mommy wants me here so I guess it can't be bad. I'll go see what this is all about.*" After a few minutes he got up from his self assigned "time out" and went and joined the circle. The teacher smiled and said she was happy he joined them and he actually smiled in return. *I turned and left having no clue that I had just witnessed the initial indicator that my son and traditional education might not get along.*

We have another baby, this time a girl. He is the best big brother ever. Her first words were not mama or dada. Oh no, she said "my Jacob." A tad bit disappointing but how can I blame her? He is an awesome kid.

Kindergarten comes and goes. He is starting to play sports and he's really good. The left handed kid can throw far. Everyone says he is a "natural athlete." The relatives come to all his games and cheer loudly and are so excited at his performance. He laughs his little kid laugh and says, "thank you", taking the accolades in stride because he could care less. He plays because we want him to play. He does well because well, he's a "natural athlete." There is not a competitive bone in his body. I can tell, and he knows I know. He plays anyway because it makes us happy.

2000-2001

First grade and report cards: S=Satisfactory, U=Unsatisfactory. How we parents want so badly to have all S's on a report card. End of school year, his report card is fine but his teacher wants to meet. There are concerns that even though he is "academically ready" he doesn't seem to be "socially ready" and it is "strongly recommended" that he is "held back." I took it personally and that was my first mistake. "My kid is smart," you said so yourself. "He is happy and kind and helpful." I was able to justify it. Isn't it true that girls mature faster than boys? He was a young five when he started Kindergarten. Should he have waited until he was six? If an extra year now will gain him needed social skills and will help him in the long run.... hmmmmmm, what to do, what to do.

2001-2002

The explanation went like this, "Jake, mommy made a mistake in starting you in school too early. You didn't do anything wrong. I was over excited about school for you but should have waited one more year before you started. It's not your fault, it's mine." His response was a simple, "okay". But it it wasn't ok. This feeling is unknown to me; a feeling of being judged by the successes (or failures) of my child.

I come from a family of educators. I myself am certified in secondary education (9-12). However, I am not a K-5 educator. It is not my skill set and I won't pretend that it is. They are the experts. I never thought to push back; tell me more specifically what "socially not ready" means. I never thought to challenge how he is outside of school in comparison to what he is (or isn't in this case) inside of school. I wanted what was best for him and would do anything to make sure my kid was successful. If this was their recommendation, then so be it. He repeated

1st grade. *This was my 2nd indicator that my son and traditional education might not get along.*

A work sheet comes home from school that needs to be done over. No note, no directions, apparently he didn't get it right the first time so he gets another chance. I'm assuming that means he needs help? The single piece of paper has a picture of coins; quarter, dime, nickel and penny. The paper has been copied so many times the images aren't very clear and really vague instructions aren't very helpful either. I call this 1 dimensional (1D) learning. It's common practice to rely on "paper based" tools. A school can't walk around with loose change everywhere. Except I know that he is a 3 dimensional (3D) learner. He won't understand how to count money if this is how he is being taught.

"Get the jar of change in the closet please and dump it all on the carpet", I said. We sit criss-cross applesauce and get ready for a lesson. "Dig your hand in the pile. Lift the coins up and let them fall through your fingers over and over again. (FEEL it). Count out 25 of the pennies. These are worth 1¢ each" I say. He does it. "All of this together is 25 cents. I hate carrying around all these coins. They are heavy and jingle so I'd like to carry around fewer coins. Let's trade those 25 pennies in for fewer coins that equal the same amount." I pick out five nickels. We continue to do the 'trade out for less' concept using 2 dimes and a nickel (3 coins) and finally a quarter (1 coin). I give him random numbers: 88, 72, 91, 34 cents and allow him to always start with whatever number of coins he wants. Many times we do the "trade out for less" to understand that carrying the least amount of coins is usually preferred. We even figured out how to take all that change and trade it for paper money (dollar bills). When all is said and done we have $9.33. I asked "Does that make sense/cents?" He laughed and his eyes were bright. "YES!" "Perfect, because all that money is yours. Since you could count it you can keep it. Take what you learned and apply it to that piece of paper." He did, and he got it all right.

Looking back there were many times I "re-taught the lesson" using hands-on, or physically building something to get the message across. I have no idea how I knew what to do at the time. I'm just thankful that I did. But deep down, it really bothered me.

2003

Jacob is having trouble reading. We buy Hooked on Phonics®. We work our way through every book and put the *stickers of success* on the chart. I tell myself that reading "will click." He will find his groove. I have to be honest; this is new territory for me. I'm not exactly sure what I'm doing. I don't remember how I learned to read, I just did it. I was ordinary. Everything about me is ordinary. I'm only prepared for ordinary. I keep telling myself to have faith that everything will be okay.

Walking through the mall during the holidays I come across a kiosk with an Asian gentleman who creates the most beautiful art. I ask him to make me three signs using his alphabet for my "P" words: patience, passion and purpose. He has to write it in English on the back of each sign so I know which is which. I have them matted and framed. I'll hang them in my home office.

Jacob sees the picture frames in my room and asks what they are. "Patience" I begin, "is because sometimes I want everything all at once. I need to slow down and appreciate what I have and know that I will have all that I want. But I need to have patience. Passion is because I want to love what I do. Everyone should have something that they are passionate about. Something that brings them such joy and happiness they couldn't imagine their life without it. And Purpose..." is where he jumps in and interrupts me to yell, "that one is easy! Your purpose is to be my mom!" I smile and hug him. I'm glad he provided an answer because my response would have been *I'm really not sure what my purpose is*. He's eight.

In his world, Mom is unwavering support. Mom gives him hugs and kisses and tells him all the things he deserves to hear. We cuddle at night to read books like Harry Potter out loud. He loves how Mom reads. He tells me all the time I'm a really good reader. I realize that when we do this together (he helps me with words and we discuss to reiterate understanding) this mom/son activity needs to stay separate from teacher/student activities. We have a conflict. I stop teaching him to read using Hooked on Phonics®.

Sylvan Learning Centers: 4 days a week, every week, after school. He never complains. What long days he has. He worked hard. His tutors loved him. He bulldozed his way through and somehow learned a method that was sufficient to read and remember. Let's throw some math in too since he's already onsite anyway. Oh, and let's not worry about the fact that we just spent his freshman year of college tuition to get through the 4th grade. *This was my 3rd indicator that my son and traditional education might not get along.*

FEBRUARY 2005

The kids have been complaining that I travel too much for work. I try to explain that the economy in Michigan isn't the best. If they want me to be home more we will need to move; preferably somewhere warm. They immediately think mommy will go work for Disney® (their idea of warm). They don't yet understand how hard it can be to find employment. On a personal note, I started reading things I don't normally read such as *Illusions: The Adventures of a Reluctant Messiah* by Richard Bach (Random House, 1977) and *The Alchemist* by Paulo Coelho (Harper Collins, 1998). I was a trashy romance novel kind of girl. As my mind opened, I found my way to *The Law of Attraction* by Esther and Jerry Hicks (Hay House, Inc., September 2006). How hard can it be to figure out what I want? How naïve. But one thing was really quite simple. I want what is best for my kids. Warm weather, comparable cost of living to the Midwest, good public school and tech industry: we moved to Austin, Texas.

Checking them into the new school with only 3 months left in the school year was a challenge. School assessments indicated both kids were "behind." The school staff is concerned as to how to bring the kids up to par (to their standards) before the school year ends. Back to Sylvan, this time **both** kids. Seriously, what am I missing?

They love Sylvan. With a 3-to-1 student to teacher ratio I love it too. But if Sylvan is really working, why am I not seeing the results "long term?" I understand the high student-to-teacher ratio in public schools these days. But why would <u>both</u> my kids have the same difficulties? If it is not the education system, it <u>has</u> to be the kids. This school district, luckily, suggested testing them both for learning disabilities (I have no idea why Sylvan didn't also make this suggestion). His testing did not indicate any quantifiable challenges, but hers did.

The school attempts to 'match' the student with a teacher vs. just random placement. I'm sure other schools do this as well. It was nice to know that there was some thought put into it. He was placed with a veteran educator who was very nurturing and "grandma-ish". He excelled in her 5th grade class and needed no outside assistance. I can only guess that he felt so comfortable with her and wanted to please her, so he did. He left elementary school passing the state tests with an above average or "exemplary" status (I have no clue what that meant) in his core classes. He's acclimated to being here. He has a great group of grade school boys he hangs out with and the chance to meet more kids in 6th grade is appealing. Things are looking up.

2006-2007

Welcome to middle school with different teachers for different subjects. It requires being organized, being flexible, willing to speak up if the instructions are not clear (no coddling here). Most of all, it requires finding your "niche" amongst all those kids from all those schools that are now consolidated.

Remember how mean kids can be if you look different (are different)? Heaven forbid if a kid is overweight, shy, too short or too tall. Not fitting in can be difficult. He rarely sees his 5th grade friends. Everyone has been split up.

He has a very strong sense of self yet he is very modest, humble even. He doesn't show off. He actually doesn't like to draw attention to himself, which in turn unfortunately, draws attention. Overall, he liked his teachers and did well. His 6th grade science project even won in his grade. The project was eligible for admissions to the city level fair (it was pretty cool). Demonstrates creativity? Yes.

The ability to go with the flow and do what is expected to be done in class starts to decline. It intensified with a teacher who didn't seem very happy. This person taught history which is Jake's favorite subject. It was evident (to me anyway) that this man probably shouldn't be teaching anymore. I felt his negativity immediately at our first meeting. It was almost like Jake couldn't shake this man's vibe. I believe it was the beginning of his ability to discern the teachers that really wanted to be there from the ones that were only going through the motions. He was always respectful and polite; never received a negative comment about his attitude. Report card comments started coming in that he "doesn't hand in homework" or "performs poorly on tests." If he was trying to play a game, he was not going to win. He started failing classes. Self-imposed isolation slowly creeps in.

2009

I spend many hours being a self proclaimed secretary/ administrative assistant trying to keep him organized and "on task." It was exhausting and frustrating. He spent the summer after 8th grade in summer school retaking a few subjects in order to advance to high school (9th grade). Summer school was easy (small class size, focused effort). I knew for a fact that aptitude was not the problem. There was something bigger going on and I was going to figure out what it was. Yet another unknown feeling for me surfaces: anxiety.

Let's be frank. I am a control freak. I have extremely high expectations of myself which in turn means I have high expectations of others (I'm working on it). Total panic has not yet set in. I am going to approach this like any other problem that is posed to me. I'll solution design the hell out of it until I make it work. I am an avid reader and luckily I can read fast. I'm not afraid to ask questions and I'm not afraid to ask for help. The challenge was who to ask and also be able to clearly articulate what I was asking. I found my research wasn't just about my kids. It was also about me. I questioned my ability to be a good parent; to be the right kind of parent that my kids needed. Trust me, for someone that has always been able to get from point A to point B in no time flat self doubt is not an attractive look on me.

I'm meeting amazing people in our new city and made the most incredible friends. All of us are transplants from somewhere else trying to make a home for ourselves where immediate family doesn't reside. Interestingly, most of my new friends didn't have children. Yet mine were embraced and accepted along with unsolicited observations. "You have WONDERFUL kids." "I wish I had a mom like you." "I love spending time with your daughter. She makes me feel like a kid again without feeling like an idiot." And finally, "Your son is a very old soul. He's so calming and interesting to talk to." Old soul? I've thought and said that exact same thing many times. He reminded me of an old man in a kid body. I've even said it out loud to him. He'd grin and say, "Maybe!"

This quest to find answers was making me a known face at the local Barnes & Nobel® (and costing me a lot of money). I have quite an extensive library now and of course friends would share books they thought would be of interest to me. Every day I felt like I was drawing closer and closer. My personal growth was really starting to branch out to how my own life's decisions were impacting my kids. I re-read *Ask and It is Given: Learning to Manifest Your Desires* by Esther and Jerry Hicks (Hay House, Inc. October 2004). Why do I keep coming back to this book? "Keep fear of the unknown out of it Arnette" I tell myself over and over.

2009-2010

Freshman year in high school was everything we did not want it to be. He tried to find his place but it just wasn't happening.

No more band. Still no desire to play sports (a competitive nature was a necessity now). He tried ROTC for a semester. I spent more time at the school than I had time to spare. He readily agreed to show up early for tutoring, stay during lunch, stay after school. Tutoring meant he couldn't ride the bus and had to be driven to and from school. Luckily I worked remotely (didn't have to be in an office) and had flexible hours. His weight had been steadily climbing since middle school. He became withdrawn and only wanted to play video games. He had a few close friends but even they seemed to be fading away. "They like different things," he would say.

He started to lie. Our frustrations exploded into screaming matches. How can he still be failing with all the tutoring? How can homework not be finished if ....wait a minute...did he even GO to tutoring? Do I have to actually WALK you to class? I couldn't trust what he was saying. Who is this person? This is not my kid. My same questions were given the same answer. "I don't know. I don't know why I do what I do or don't do what I'm supposed to do. It's like I check out. Like I'm there but I'm not there!" and the agony in his voice made it true. His sister was paralyzed by what she was witnessing. Some people said "Let him fail. Maybe that's what he needs." My job as his mother is to not let that happen. This is not my kid. This is not our life. Please God, help me. "Take a deep breath" I told myself. It's time to get outside of my comfort zone.

I seek out an Astrologer[2]. How lucky we are that this science can be shared by the masses! Though a random meeting is not so random, I still don't share this with my family. I'm afraid of their judgment. It provided direction for me, especially professionally. It was a stepping stone where each event opens the door to a new life experience.

I met with other spiritual advisors. I learned a little bit more here and there, which all led me to meet with a Life Path Healer/Intuitive Life Coach[3]. Within the first 5 minutes together she said the words that changed my life. Mind you, this woman knows nothing about me (except my name, email address and that we had an appointment at 1:00 pm). "Oh!" she said with a huge smile on her face, "Your son is Indigo[4]." My mind is racing...Indigo? What the heck is that? "Oh my!" she said, "and your daughter is Indigo too. {chuckling} What were you thinking to agree to two Indigo Children? You have your work cut out for you!" *This was the 4th indicator that my son and traditional education might not get along.*

Indigo Children. My life will never be the same.

---

[2]   Astrologer–Laura Waldman http://www.laurawaldmanastrology.com

[3]   Linda Drake – Life Path Healer/Intuitive Life Coach http://lindadrakeconsulting.com

[4]   Indigo Child – one who displays a new and unusual set of psychological attributes and shows a pattern of behavior generally undocumented before. Lee Carrol, Jan Tober, *The Indigo Children: The New Kids Have Arrived* (Hay House, Inc., 1999).

I kept reminding myself this was not a medical diagnosis but rather a spiritual diagnosis. I didn't care. Everything I've learned up to this point has brought me to this place. I devoured anything and everything I could get my hands on regarding Indigo Children. Some books were too clinical. Some books were just too far "out there." The best resource at the time (for me anyway) is *"The Care and Feeding of Indigo Children"* by Doreen Virtue (Hay House Publishing, 2001). The product description for the book is as follows:

> *Indigo Children are bright, intuitive, strong-willed, and sometimes self destructive individuals. They are often labeled (and misdiagnosed) as having ADD or ADHD because they won't comply with established rules and patterns; and they may exhibit behavioral problems at home and at school...*

I was mesmerized. This made sense. I read that book in the parking lot of the store. Finally, I had an understanding of what I've been dealing with (and no I am not crazy). There are many opinions out there regarding the definition and validity of Indigo. We may or may not agree on all points. Based on my personal experiences, I cannot fit a round peg (my kids) into a square hole (traditional education). I refuse to say square peg in around hold because my kids are not "square."

I am not here to confirm, nor deny (or even excuse) the classification of Indigo. I find it ironic that public education will readily support numerous programs funded by tax payer dollars for "gifted" children. I could argue that my children are "gifted" as well, just not in the one dimensional way we currently use to identify who is, or is not, gifted. He is *really intelligent*. That was never disputed. The ability to "apply one's self" and be "assessed via the recognized methods" unfortunately don't coincide with the way he performs. Let me very clear. It is a choice, his choice, on whether he chooses to perform or not. He may acknowledge what you ask, though it doesn't guarantee he will execute what you are asking. He's more interested in *why* you are asking it? *How* are you asking it? Since he has no quantifiable "learning disability" (i.e. though common characteristics of Indigo he is not ADD or ADHD) I at least now have some semblance of an explanation; and I believe it to be true.

MAY 2010

The final meeting with his 9th grade "team" went exactly as anticipated. He was contrite. Actually embarrassed that here we are, again, to discuss his inability to be like the normal teenager. I was honest with him "They will imply that it's your fault. They will position it that they've given you every opportunity and you just didn't deliver. You are a good kid, Jake. You are loving, smart, funny, loving (did I say that already?). Everything a mother could want in their kid."

I arrived at the meeting not in the casual attire (which I normally wear and is common while living in this overheated state). Rather, I dressed like the Director of Learning & Development for a Fortune 100 company that I was. With my Bachelor's Degree in Business Education and my Master's Degree in Human Resources tucked inside my brain, I would not be intimidated. Instead of sliding into a seat, I purposely positioned myself at the head of the table with him to my left. We've met so many times before yet they looked at me differently. I looked back at them the same. I listened.

Their arguments were just as I suspected and I wouldn't dispute anything they said. He didn't do the work. The fact that he passed their standardized tests at the end of the year was the ultimate outcome the district wanted. But in the end, he didn't have the credits to advance to 10th grade. He'd have to do summer school again. He sat quietly with his hands in his lap, his head bowed down. Finally, as I knew it would (you can sugar coat it as much as you want) it got personal. "Jake, really, {insert huge exasperated sigh} you shouldn't have to come early or stay after school anyway for tutoring. There is no reason why you couldn't get all your work done during the day or with a little bit of extra effort at home. The other kids can get their work done in plenty of time. The curriculum is proven and the amount of homework is monitored. It's just that you don't do what you are supposed to do. You don't apply yourself." I looked at Jake; the tears had not yet come. A 15 year old boy in a man's body yet he still looked very small. He lifted his head and spoke very clearly, just as he did when he was 3. "Actually Mr. X, I really appreciated the extra effort each of my teachers spent with me to give me the one-on-one time that I needed. I know that you are all busy and the last thing you wanted to do was to take the little bit of free time you have outside of class and spend it with me. I did improve on my homework but between that and my poor quiz scores it was too little too late. All in all, I am proud of the improvements that I made and I thank you for that {insert their blank stares all around}." Talk about an eloquent statement from the kid who can't pass English.

His counselor slid the papers in front of me to sign up for summer classes. I said "Thank you, but that won't be necessary." She looked at me, confused. Jake looked at me, confused as well. I gathered my things. Shook hands with a few people near me and thanked them for their time. Jake scooted out of his seat and stood next to me. I squeezed his arm and smiled a genuine smile. "He won't be back for 10th grade. We'll be looking into alternative approaches to education from this point forward." We were both done with being judged. *It was the 5th and final time, as I knew my son and traditional education <u>definitely</u> did not get along.*

JUNE 2010-JUNE 2011

Finding alternative methods of education isn't as easy as it sounds. We found Kaplan College Prep® (online education) originally intended for kids who lived overseas and/or were athletes or theater kids. Kaplan worked around their various schedules. What I loved about this program was he had 12 weeks to finish class and he wasn't required to take more than 1 at a time. Additionally, he could speed through all the content and finish early if he wanted. It was soon apparent that if he only had 1 or 2 things to concentrate on, it was doable (mind you, there was music, phone/texting, email, social media all going on at the same time too). Unlike multiple subjects all day, every day. Though he barely passed Spanish I (traditionally) he flew through Spanish II in 8 weeks earning a solid C. Would an A or B be preferred? Absolutely. But Spanish II is hard especially with a poor foundation...we'll take it! The obvious negative, if there had to be one, was Kaplan was not "recognized by the state" as a "valid alternative" to earn his high school diploma. Basically, if we tried to re-enroll him into high school none of the Kaplan credits would be accepted. It was a big risk but I vowed he'd never go back.

Slowly but surely the self esteem and confidence came back. Because I mostly worked from home it was easy to monitor when he was dedicating time to school online. Did he wander? Did I catch him watching YouTube® videos? Yes. But overall, he was in control of what was happening. That was important.

As a 16 year old with a driving license he was able to run errands for me any time during "normal school hours" (the joy of access to his schooling 24 hours a day). He was a night owl and preferred to do his schoolwork later. Friends who traveled for work appreciated the fact he could drive dogs to/from the kennel with no time restrictions. He could pick up his sister from volleyball or basketball practice. He could go grocery shopping or get the car washed. He was able to work a few hours a month as an IT Intern at his dads' office. At 16, he felt productive. He was productive!

Did I worry that he wasn't around kids his own age? Constantly. Yet, I also had to be honest that he never really cared for kids his own age anyway. The social hierarchy of high school was a foreign concept to him. He never understood the meaning of popularity and cliques; all of it "was stupid." He was happy. He was doing the work. We had found the solution. Or had we?

AUGUST 2011

I've committed to a healthier lifestyle and taking better care of my mind, body and soul. Out are random massages at whatever spa had a price special. Instead, I embraced Acupuncture and Oriental Medicine[5]. I need to be able to keep not only myself, but my children, balanced and healthy. I receive my First and Second Degree attunements in USUI Reiki[6]. I continue to meditate, write in a journal and sit with my Angel Cards almost every night. I shake my head in wonder. What a crazy path I'm on right now.

---

[5]   Acupuncture and Oriental Medicine – Cindy Nilson http://www. cindynilson.com

[6]   Reiki is the universal art of natural healing that positively affects the whole person including the body, emotions, mind and spirit.

SEPTEMBER 2011

The bills are mounting. Kaplan is expensive. His 529 college fund cannot be used for tuition. It was no different than if we had decided to send him to private school. Options, I want options. It seems the universe is always looking out for me. As I continued to worry about the costs, I received a call from them. It seems Kaplan was bought by a larger conglomerate (weird word used in regards to education). K12.com®, a large online solution, purchased the smaller Kaplan and was "discontinuing the program as it currently exists." Well, we LIKE the program as it currently exists. The K12 program wasn't a good fit, which is why I went with Kaplan in the first place. Easy answer for me, if it didn't exist, then I don't have to pay for it anymore. (Note: K12.com is now acknowledged as a *free* alternative to traditional public education. It was not for us in 2009). I wasn't looking forward to researching more schools. In addition, the novelty of "online" was wearing off. He's easily bored. I always do my best problem solving when I sleep. It seems I always find my answer in my dreams.

I called my mother who is a retired high school administrator. "What can you tell me about getting a GED[7]? Do you have to

---

[7] General Education Development (or GED) test(s) are used for educational testing services designed to provide a high school equivalency credential. http://www.merriam-webster.com/dictionary/ged

be 18 and a high school dropout in order to qualify?" I asked. I'm sure I must have totally caught her off guard. GED has negative connotations associated with it. It aligned with... failure. I am embarrassed to say that I was embarrassed (about what was happening to us). I'm fortunate that my parents have always been there for me. I know that is one of the reasons I'm fighting so hard to be there for Jake. I can say without hesitation, that I would do anything to change the direction from this path we've found ourselves on.

Thank goodness for Google®. Did you know that a person at the age of 16 or 17 can take the GED tests with parent consent? Did you know that most community colleges will accept a GED just like a high school diploma? It might be difficult to get into a university with only a GED. However, after earning an Associate Degree you could then transfer into a university. Did you know that the GED actually consists of five different tests that must be passed individually and on a total average? We also learned that the cost of taking the GED would be less than $100! It may not be "main stream" but it is legal. I felt empowered. Plan B has been found.

He signed up. He could attend preparation courses through our local community education program or through the community college. Instead, we purchased study guides. After which I remembered that "study" doesn't really align with him. Just do it. Try it. If you pass the first time, outstanding! If not, then the study guides might help. Test #1 History (his favorite):

PASSED. Test #2 Science: PASSED. Test #3 Reading: PASSED. Test #4 and #5....the results never came. Never came and never came. Odd.

When push comes to shove (mothers intuition?), it's kind of hard to lie your way out of it. Especially when the testing center can verify he never even scheduled it. Why not? FEAR of failure. FEAR of success. The goal was to have all the tests done by end of year (let's not drag this out). But now the testing center was shut down for the holidays. Regret. Apologetic. Valid emotions that could have been avoided (says the adult to the teenager) if you had just talked to me. I'm here to help you. It's okay to be afraid of the unknown. Don't you know this by now? I call in the big guns. I reach into my tool chest of everything I've learned. Talk to your Angels kiddo. Call in Archangel Metatron[8] who lovingly aids the Indigo Child. Ask them to help you remember what you need to know when you need to know it. You can do this.

---

8   Doreen Virtue PhD., Guidebook for Archangel Oracle Cards, (Hay House Publishing 2004). Archangel Metatron works closely with Indigo and Crystal children.

JANUARY 2012

An envelope comes in the mail addressed to him. I of course open it because, well, I'm the mom. The State of (blah blah blah) proudly recognizes (blah blah blah) and presents (blah blah blah) High School Equivalency...GED. I assume that means he passed Test #4 Math and Test #5 Writing? Outstanding! So much for the GED study guides. They have been donated to the local library.

The Life Path Healer/Intuitive Life Coach has played a pivotal role in my life and I feel she will do the same for Jake. We made an appointment which never would have found its way on her schedule if the timing was not right. Though I'm in the room, I can see the connection is between the two of them. I'm just a fly on the wall. She acknowledges the Indigo Child and is honored to be working with one with such a high vibration. She explains everything so much better than I ever could. Is he relieved? Yes. Is he hesitant? Yes.

Our Spirit Guides and Angels are proud that I was willing and able to help my kid. I asked for assistance and I "listened" when ideas popped into my head. I followed divine guidance. They acknowledged that during high school he did indeed "mentally check out" for lack of a better term. Though his human body sat there, his higher self did not "stay grounded;" it left him. High school was boring. *Walk into class. Sit in a tiny chair; too many people, too much energy (some good, some bad), judgment; so much judgment. I'll just leave for a little while. I'll come back when it's time to move to the next classroom in a box. WHY? Why stay in this physical space when I can be UP THERE?*

Did it make sense? Yes. What did I feel? Relief.

JUNE 2012

It's summer. Six months since the GED was earned. He's been keeping busy. Most of the "soon-to-be high school seniors" are hanging around enjoying their time off, probably thinking of the upcoming school year. They've filled out the career counselor's questionnaire. Do their abilities and interests coincide with being an accountant, engineer or mechanic? Did they score well on their ACT/SAT tests? What to wear for senior pictures? Who will I go to prom with? Or, are they planning graduation and family celebrations? My boy won't be among them.

Jake skipped over all that. He started college today when he actually should be starting 12th grade. Though, his purpose won't ever be listed on a career counselor's questionnaire. I have no clue what our next steps are, but at least we are "free" to pursue anything and everything. I will continue to think outside of the box and pay attention to the signs as they present themselves. I'm sure there is so much more to come.

Note how quickly everything accelerates now.

JULY 2012

I sit at my parent's cabin in the woods of Northern Michigan. The words flow into what I finally call an "essay." It's not enough information to be a book. Maybe a short story I can submit to Readers Digest. Maybe it was just meant for me and the few close friends I feel safe to share it with. They've seen me struggle over the years trying to figure out what is going on, not only with Jake but his sister as well. My fears about Jake have turned to nervous anticipation; knowing my work is not yet done. I still have to help him find a career path. I have new fears for Erynn, his 14 year old sister who starts 9th grade this year. She's Indigo as well with a dyslexic flair (that's a new challenge I didn't have before). I'm more prepared this time around, but she's very different than her brother.

In 4th grade Erynn received a dyslexic diagnosis and she was provided 504 accommodations[9]. In her case, she can read. She just can't remember what she has read. If we read to her out loud, she can recall the information. She does her homework (unlike her brother) and is very creative, so projects are easy. Unfortunately, Erynn can't test. No matter how big (state

---

[9] Section 504 is part of the Rehabilitation Act of 1973 that prohibits discrimination based upon disability. Section 504 is an anti-discrimination, civil rights statute that requires the needs of students with disabilities to be met as adequately as the needs of the non-disabled are met. (http://www.greatschools.org/special-education/legal-rights/868-section-504.gs).

mandated tests) or how small (quizzes) she just cannot manage the pencil to paper process.

I encourage every parent to leverage the programs within their district to test for a "medical diagnosis" because it is the only thing that is going to help you "within" the educational system. You need that assessment to push for assistance and don't be afraid to ask for it. Truth be told, I was embarrassed at first, which I now realize is ridiculous. This is not about me, this is about my child. If that little "504" is going to make a difference, you bet I'm going to use it. They will reassess at the end of every school year. Hang on to it for as long as you can. A district receives more funding because of that status, so leverage it. Not all teachers are well versed in 504 guidelines so be sure to understand what your child's options are. As your child moves from grade to grade, do not assume their needs are clearly communicated, especially when transitioning from elementary school to junior high to high school.

Have a clear understanding of what works and doesn't work. We've learned that she performs well with teachers that are dynamic lecturers. Unfortunately, not all teachers are engaging storytellers, nor does class time really allow for that every day. "Quiet learning" doesn't penetrate her brain like an amazing dialog. I'm keeping my fingers crossed that her high school experience will be different than her brothers.

AUGUST 2012

The high school experience is not different than her brothers. I think I read it somewhere, or maybe it was just implanted in my brain, that Indigo children around 10th grade, finally succumb to the traditional rigors of high school. More often than not, they drop out. Our strategy: keep the homework grades really high so when testing time comes she has wiggle room. It's not as easy as it sounds.

It's not just dealing with the academics. It is the social aspects that are shifting. She used to be involved in sports (for the interaction of it, not because she really cared about winning). At first an injury kept her from playing (a blessing in disguise I think). Then it was realizing the schedule was too intense and she wouldn't be able to maintain her grades and play at the same time. Then it was self-imposed isolation that started to creep in. She always liked her alone time but now it was with music playing non-stop. The girls she hung out with since 6th grade aren't including her anymore. When I ask if it bothers her she says "No, it's my choice, not theirs." With Jake, I tried to push "being social" but now I know better. I allow her this time to just "be." She's not a typical teenage girl that wants to go to football games and dances, to the mall or to parties. A different child, a different gender, but the signs are all the same.

As part of her 504 compliance status, I meet with her counselor and actively communicate with her teachers. I push for, and get, an Oral Accommodation Level II allowing for the entire test being read out loud if she chooses. She really hates being different. She's very frustrated that no matter how hard she tries this isn't going to get any better. I found an alternative for Jake with the GED tests. But I cannot give parent consent for that until she is 16. She's got to hang in there through 10th grade. Even then, she can't paper/pencil test, so I don't know what our options are going to be. I can only reassure her (and myself) over and over again, I <u>will</u> figure something out. I continue to meet weekly with my friend Karen Viotto for lunch. She's a Biology Professor but more so, an amazing (and animated) lecturer. She has had many students over the years that she now assumes are Indigo. We brainstorm constantly as to what improvements could be made to accommodate different learning styles. In addition she's helped me tremendously in my spiritual journey. "Wouldn't it be nice" I say, "if GED tests were computerized and had an oral component to them? It would be a dream come true."

Angel Card: Brilliant Idea: build a website. I give myself five years to develop a support forum for the parents and guardians of Indigo children. Yet it's not only a website. It will be a database of profiles, Indigo profiles. As a parent I'd like to find and read about other Indigo children based on certain criteria. Maybe based on age or 504 attributes, hobbies or habits. Yes, it's all mapped out in my head. It's on my to-do list.

OCTOBER 2012

My home office phone is ringing which is not uncommon since I work from home. The caller ID displays the name of Linda Drake. Odd, I thought. Is Jake late for an appointment? It is out of the ordinary for Linda to be calling me. "Hello?" I answered. "Hello Arnette. This is Linda Drake." She cut right to the chase. "I have a woman in session right now and your name came up. Apparently you know something or someone that can help her with her business. Do you mind giving her a call?" she asked. "Um, sure, okay" I said. I let two days pass and I called and left a message. Something like, "Hi. My name is Arnette. Linda Drake asked me to call indicating that I might be able to help you with a work issue. Yeah... thanks, bye" (feeling just a tad bit awkward). We played phone tag, but we eventually connected. She was the owner of a local business looking to hire her #2 person. Literally, within two minutes the name "Dan Viotto" popped into my head. Clear as day. I interrupted her and said, "I think I know your person. I don't even know if he's looking for a job, but I'll ask him." There was excitement in her voice. "You know my person?" she asked. "Yes....yes, I think I do."

Long story short, she and my friend Dan connected and Dan did indeed work with her for a while as her #2 person. (I believe because I was eventually going to need website development services[10].) There you have it Arnette (I say to myself), tangible

---

[10] www.goindigohealing.com

proof for your logical brain that you "hear." It has been a fun story to tell but it gets so much better.

NOVEMBER 2012

Jake is 18. Now he thinks he'll study criminal justice in his hopes to become a trainer in a police canine unit. In addition, he's received his USUI Reiki I and II degree attunements from Linda Drake. We feel this will compliment his career choice; being able to provide healing to the dogs. Jake is volunteering at the local animal shelter administering Reiki on animals. Any assistance with emotional and physical healing will help in placing the animals in a foster home or with a permanent adoption. Linda talks to me about him spending time with specialists in the field of animal communication. "He could do it now, but after Reiki III he will be better" she says. I make a mental note, maybe someday. We are also considering approaching a local dog training school for a possible internship after graduation. That seems like the next logical step.

DECEMBER 2012

The drive home to Michigan for the holiday was eye opening for all of us. I not only feel understood but also have a sense of peace. Years ago when I didn't feel I could share that I was seeking help from an astrologer (let alone a life coach) this statement was music to my ears. "Arnette, let me be clear. It's not the fact that you went to see an astrologer. It's the fact that **YOU** went to see an astrologer." I laugh in agreement. How accurate that observation is to all that knew me before Indigo was part of my life. How I live my life now seems like such a natural extension of who, and what, I am. What is, or is not, *logical*, no longer defines me.

In Michigan, Jacob spends time with his Aunt Carrie at her equestrian center. She took on the care of a neglected horse, Frankie, who had been plagued with nothing but illness and injury since coming to her barn. Initially, an estimated 300 pounds under weight when arriving, he was finally almost healthy. Carrie asked Jacob to spend time with Frankie because he seemed melancholy. Even though he was very well cared for and loved.

Jacob is afraid of horses. He certainly didn't know what to expect. His uncle brought Frankie into the large (but cold) indoor arena. Jacob stood, just steps away from a very intimidating thoroughbred horse. When he raised his hands in front of him, Frankie would back away. When he would put his hands down, Frankie would walk forward. Jacob could not get close enough to Frankie to administer Reiki. So they agreed to "just talk."

Jacob called his aunt on the cell phone and said, "He wants to run. I'm not sure what that means. He wants to run and that's why he's been so sad." Surprised? Yes. Unbeknownst to Jacob, Frankie had been a *race horse.*

When Jacob relays this to me I of course ask "and"? In my mind (still being the logical person that I am) there has got to be a "next step." What brings Frankie joy, the physical act of running? Does he want Carrie to ride on the 4-wheeler beside him for a sense of playful competition? Does he want Carrie to sit on the railing of the pasture cheering and waving her arms yelling "go Frankie go!"? What is the feeling he is missing? You need to be able to connect the dots between the animal and the human, Jacob. Don't just stop. You need to bridge that gap so Carrie knows what she needs to do to come full circle. Good thing we go back in the summer for another "conversation." Jacob nodded his head with his "ah- ha moment." It is not just what you hear, you also need to *interpret.* What you do with the information is just as important (Dr. Doolittle in training?)

JANUARY 2013

College didn't turn out so well. Jake carried two classes during the summer. The grades suspiciously never made it home. Strangely, he was still able to register for two fall classes, and did really well...in the beginning. Then the novelty wore off. It is very difficult for Jake to find his voice, primarily because he so desperately doesn't want to disappoint anyone. If I come to him and pose the questions, he will open up. It is a work in progress for him to understand that not speaking up about what he feels or thinks is more destructive (to everyone) in the long run. Until then, it's apparently still part of my job to figure it out and present it back to him. I'm exhausted.

As one door closes another opens up. The timing of all of this is unbelievable. With college out of the question (for now), so is a degree in criminal justice and K9 dogs. Jake is accepted in an apprenticeship program with a national dog training school (the same place he previously thought he might intern with after graduation). We are anticipating this trainer credential will be more "understood and accepted" by society. (He can slip the Reiki healing in on the side.) His long term goal: rehabilitative services (emotional and physical balance) for working animals such as military, search & rescue, and police dogs, maybe even horses. Where do I come up with this stuff? Is that even a real job?

My current customer is requesting me to be onsite to deliver training. Not the London or New York office, but Iowa City. It's February, and it's cold. Not my ideal work trip. I meet a woman who works for Pearson VUE which offers innovative computer-based testing solutions through secure, electronic test delivery. They provide a full suite of services from test development to data management, to deliver exams through the world's most comprehensive and secure network of test centers in 175 countries. On break, I casually ask if they do anything with GED®. Her face lights up and says "Oh, my gosh.

It's actually quite amazing. We partnered with the American Council of Education to provide all GED testing online in all jurisdictions (except Canada)." I think my eyes popped out of my head. *I was sent to Iowa City to connect with this person about the GED®.* Thank you!

When Jacob took the GED® it was old fashioned pencil and paper testing and manually graded. The results took weeks to get back. The authoring tools used today to create online content and assessment tests are amazingly interactive. It's exactly what this generation of young adults need. But, more than that, with Erynn's "valid medical diagnosis" and 504 accommodations, the tests can be administered orally over headsets! The online testing is available in January 2014. She turns 16 February 2014. Fingers crossed, I believe I just found her Plan B if traditional education doesn't work out.

For more information regarding GED® and online testing please visit **www.gedtestingservice.com**

FEBRUARY 2013

I've been feeling like I need to see Linda Drake again. It has been awhile and it helps me have these touch points with her and Abraham, along with my own Angels and Spirit Guides. Over the years, I've read many wonderful books by Esther and Jerry Hicks. As with Esther Hicks, Linda has been blessed to work with Abraham as well. I cover the same discussion points every time: my son, my daughter (both Indigo), my parents, my work, myself. I remind myself to schedule an appointment; it may take awhile for an opening. In addition, I think I need to take Reiki III training so I have a better understanding of what Jacob will be able to do. I can't just sign up. I need to be invited to participate. I think I might be pushing my skill set just a little bit.

It's Saturday. I have an hour before I need to pick up my daughter. I can either a) do some work, or b) meditate. It's been a long time since I've really meditated. No one is home, no distractions. I settle in for what hopes to be a good session. Maybe I'll see my Teacher Guide (Chief) who is always a beautiful red. Maybe I'll see black and white photographs flip through so fast I have to ask them to slow down. I always hope I experience something versus falling asleep.

My head is *hurting.* I think this is what a migraine feels like though I've never had a migraine so I'm not sure. I see the most amazing metallic shimmering gold. I think to myself "Gold. I wonder where my red is?" And then I hear "it." So clear, just like I did before. It's not a sound. It's not even really a voice. It's just the words *"We gave you Dan Viotto."* (Remember my friend Dan? He ended up working with a lady because my name had come up in her session.) Startled? Definitely! My response, *"Who's we?"* *"We are Abraham."* Holy smokes! What is happening right now? I can feel one tear slide down my right cheek. I was very aware of that one tear. I had so many questions, but I was also so scattered. This is some of what I remember:

Arnette: *You gave me Dan Viotto because I needed tangible proof that what I was "hearing" was real.*

Abraham: *Of course*

Arnette: *Jake really needed a car, did we do the right thing in getting him a new car?*

Abraham: *Jacob required reliable transportation to do his work.*

Arnette: *I'm very interested in past life regression. I think that is something I would like to explore.*

Abraham: *Interesting, but not necessary.*

Arnette: *I would really like to see auras. I think that would be really cool.*

Abraham: *That is not your purpose.*

Arnette: *What is my purpose?*

Abraham: *To teach what you have learned; to speak the words of Abraham regarding Indigo Souls.*

Arnette: *Indigo Children?*

Abraham: *No Arnette, Indigo Souls.*

Arnette *I need to meet with Linda.*

Abraham: *Linda Drake will discuss with you how to write with us.*

Arnette: *Thank you, Abraham.*

Abraham: *You are most welcome, Arnette.*

Abraham: *Arnette, we shall speak again on Saturday.*

I awoke from meditation dumbfounded. Looking in the bathroom mirror there was not the trace of a single tear; my entire face was wet with tears. I called on a Sunday and left a message to schedule an appointment with Linda. I received a call directly from her. She's had a cancellation, can I come tomorrow? Abraham can make things happen!

We have a wonderful mentor in Linda. Jacob and I have both been invited for Reiki III. How blessed are we! I assumed it was because I will be assisting Jake with his development, but Linda says no. It's because I have to raise my own vibration to work with Abraham. I need to practice, practice, practice, giving and receiving Reiki from now until we have class. I am very excited about this amazing opportunity. I am also apprehensive. This is totally out of my comfort zone, again. I am not qualified. I am flying by the seat of my pants as it is....or, am I?

MARCH 2013

Time is going by quickly and I'm irritated. I'm not sure what I was hoping for, but it's not this. Jacob is not persistent enough to secure the limited time for private training sessions. He needs more one-on-one time with a dog and more attention from his coach. I keep reminding myself to relax. Technically he should be a senior in high school right now. He's too passive. It's taking a lot of restraint on my part to not call and say "Look, I paid the entire tuition up front. Shouldn't he be assigned to those slots first?" Let me just say for the record that his 529 college fund certainly didn't pay for Reiki training and it didn't pay for this program (either).

Warning bells are going off in my head. Jacob is skipping puppy classes. I can feel it in my gut. He didn't go. I drive over to his dads. I walk in on him gaming. Not showered, with fast food bags on the floor. What the heck? Calm down, calm down, you **know** what this is, you **know** this isn't him. My chest constricts with anxiety as I reach in my "tool chest" (the learning I've accumulated over the years but always forget I have available to me.) "Give me your pendulum"[11] he hands it over. I surround us in white light and confirm he has three negative entities[12] in his energy field. I fumble through calling in Archangel Michael first, then Archangel Raphael, then Michael again. I clear him, his room, and the house. I make him jump in the shower; pick up the trash. I'm a mess. What do I get? I get "Mom, you *really* need to work on your delivery." Seriously? Later I get a text that says "Thanks Mom, for always looking out for me. I love you."

Saturday night is date night (with Abraham), my laptop, my bed, and a lot of nervous energy. Will my head hurt again? Will I be able to hear? Will it be awkward? Will Abraham show up? Abraham did indeed show up. It's easier to type with my eyes closed, that way my logical mind doesn't interrupt trying to

---

[11] A tool commonly used by healers in order to receive a yes or no confirmation (gauged by energy) to a question that was posed.

[12] Spirits that have not yet crossed over and require source energy like found in a person or animal.

fix typos. Our first session....resulted in pages. I'm lucky I'm a fast typist. Abraham reminds me, "Pay attention to the signs, Arnette. Do not be afraid to make a change." Wiser words have never been spoken to me.

He's disengaged. Just like what happened with college. He's not actively pursuing, which means he's bored. Months ago Linda had talked to me about Jake working with and being mentored by specialists in animal communication after he becomes a Reiki Master. We both have our Reiki III training in two weeks. Dog training session (1 of 3) will wrap up at the end of the month. He has lost interest in the program because it's more online than we had realized. This really puts the responsibility on the student to schedule everything. Jacob is an addictive personality with "online" so we have controls in place so that he doesn't spend days and days gaming. The last kind of program I would have enrolled him in is "online." He does not think the way most people think. He can't self direct. We need to pull him out.

I have a heart-to-heart with the co-founder of the dog training program. I don't want to be negative about how the program is run. Though it may work for the majority of the students, I just know the "self-directed online" model doesn't work for us. What can I realistically say where she doesn't think I'm a kook? Do I dare say the word "Indigo"? Jacob had indicated she may be Reiki certified, so she may understand the idea of rehabilitative services through energy healing. It turns out

I didn't have to worry. The universe knows this program will benefit him in fulfilling his purpose, so they provided a solution. Jacob doesn't need to change. The *owner offered to change her program to accommodate him.* Excuse me? Thank you!

The trainers will work directly with me in scheduling him: private sessions, training classes, group meetings, everything goes through me. His dad and I, one of us, is always around when he's online for learning content. Every moment is arranged. He just shows up and does the work. I have been promoted from an administrative assistant to a "handler" (inside joke, like a dog handler.) I wonder, when the time comes, are we going to have to run Jake's business where his only purpose is to show up and heal? Abraham concurs, but it's not enough. *What about the other Indigo, Arnette? What about them?*

MARCH 30, 2013

My 49th birthday was two days ago. I am so happy to be 49 because I could not be doing what I'm doing, here and now, any earlier. My realization of purpose obviously was dependent on the last 18+ years of raising an Indigo Soul. It all came to fruition today as Jacob and I received our Reiki III attunement. Mine specifically, is to increase my vibration in order to collaborate more easily with Abraham.

Everything is aligned. Jacob will be busy for the next year finishing the apprenticeship program and then begin animal communication internships. Maybe Erynn will pass the end of year state mandated tests (required for graduation). If she doesn't, it's okay. Just like Jake, she won't get what she needs through traditional means. The universe has provided us with oral GED® testing services; it is just a question of if she'll need to take them.

I've been able to navigate my children (with aches, pains, bumps and bruises) through an education system that is geared toward "a norm." This is not where their story ends, but rather, this where our story begins. You see, my purpose is to help other parents and guardians navigate the dictates of this society... and make way for the Indigo Soul.

✶✶✶✶✶✶

Much has happened since the first printing of this book in August of 2013. This 2nd edition provides me the opportunity to update our readers with where Jacob is in his journey.

DECEMBER 2013

"It's time" the voice on the other end of the phone said. "I'm sorry, what?" I replied. "It's time for Jacob to work with an animal communicator. I have a friend, Karen Anderson (www.animalcommunicating.com), who lives near Spokane, WA. She's agreed to mentor Jacob for awhile as part of his development." Linda Drake called me directly to share this amazing news. Are you kidding me? How amazing!

Apparently Karen felt it was time as well else Jacob wouldn't have been invited. What an amazing woman to share her amazing gift.

JULY 2015

Jacob turns 21 this month. So much has happened over the last 6 years when I first heard the term "Indigo." Most recently, Jacob earned a certification in Basic Animal Care through the Texas Academy of Animal Control. This helped him tremendously in moving from a volunteer to a staff position at the Humane Society. He also became a Certified Euthanasia Technician. This one, I must admit, took its toll. However, he has learned so much about himself and how to deal with the world around him. For this particular situation, he took his own precautionary steps to protect all that he is.

A little over a year ago, a new addition to our Indigo (extended) village arrived in Texas. Christina Allen, founder and acting Director of the new Austin Shamanic Center (www. austinshamaniccenter.com) became an integral part in the personal development and expansion of Jacob (and me too!). Though he had already worked with Christina previously, he reached out to her again specific to this recent Euthanasia certification. In short, the boy in Jacob wants to protect all living things, especially dogs. However, the man in Jacob understands that, helping an animal cross over, is a gift.

As an advocate of animals, Jacob takes his responsibilities very seriously. As he explained to me, euthanizing an animal is not a *technique* it's a *process*. It encompasses being able to "communicate" what is happening and why it's happening in a loving and respectful way. Jacob has also said "no." When given the directive to put an animal down, he has refused. He's pulled animals off the "high risk" list and worked with them one-on-one, taking it upon himself to use his ability to mend emotional traumas. He then leverages social media to find foster or permanent homes for these dogs. If he could save every one of them, he would.

His passion for working with older animals has become paramount. Puppies can usually be adopted he claims. However, adult and senior dog care is where improvements are really needed. "No kill" shelters fill quickly. The process to get sanctioned as a no-kill shelter is tedious. Where does Jacob fit into all this now? The Indigo boy who is an Indigo man, what does he have to say about providing ongoing care for our furry friends? Keep reading. The answer is astounding.

ABRAHAM & ARNETTE COLLABORATE

(Words from Abraham)

There are many wonderful resources available that discuss the topic of Indigo Children. We must clarify that Indigo refers to a *soul*. The soul does not ever stop being Indigo. Souls come to Earth through conception and birth so naturally they begin their journey as infants and grow to adulthood. Being Indigo does not *go away.* Some writing emphasize behavior challenges such as ADD, ADHD, dyslexia and others as meaning, or "being" Indigo. They are real and identifiable attributes of personalities which may, or may not be, associated to an Indigo Soul.

We are bringing awareness now as there are many young Indigo Souls that need their parent or guardian to step into their Navigator role sooner rather than later. In this lifetime, and Indigo Soul may be aligned with another soul, whose role is to help (that Indigo) on their journey to purpose. This "other soul" has the Archetype of "Navigator." Rise above your own insecurities, stop personalizing events that are not a reflection on you. This is about a soul sent to do specific works of God. All souls are unique, just like a snowflake! Parents attempt to raise their children the same way (or similar) to the way them themselves were raised. It is frustrating for everyone involved because the Indigo Soul usually requires more patience and more understanding. They require guidance for an environment that feels wrong, is confusing, and overwhelming. These children do not need constant accolades. These children do not need to be put on a pedestal. If anything, they want (and need) space. To be left alone with their own thoughts and their own feelings. It is allowing them to grow stronger and stronger in their own vibrational skin. When they are ready, *and you will know when they are ready*; school them not in traditional academics as you know them, but rather in the *art of healing*.

How do I know if my child is Indigo? Ask

When a child is ill, a healthcare professional provides a medical diagnosis. There are qualified resources available to identify an Indigo Soul as well. By blood test? No. By assessment test? No. Indigo is in fact a "spiritual diagnosis" for lack of a better description, just as Arnette learned. There are many Light Workers (Earth Angels) that have studied behavioral characteristics that are common to Indigo which are more often than not absolutely correct. However, the most practical and effective way to know if your child is an Indigo Soul is to ask "on behalf of the child's higher self" and not to be influenced by the ego of a parent or guardian. You may wonder, "But whom do I ask?" That information is forthcoming.

Ego is not an Indigo characteristic but rather a human characteristic. Society is very competitive. Humans want their children to be the best of the best. They push for the right schools, the right activities, the right friends. Indigo Souls are not impressed with any of this, though their human ego may be persuaded to think that they are. Fear of rejection, failure, disappointment will influence the child to try and "fit in" because they want to please the parent more than it being a want or desire of their own. However, as the child matures and gains a better sense of self, stubbornness, rebellion, the inability (or willingness) to conform will over ride even their wanting to try. This bruises the parent's ego, who must find reasons as to why their children aren't the same as most other children. You seek labels to justify behavior: good, bad or indifferent. And if those labels are the slightest bit negative, you want *another* label that softens this (imagined) blow.

The Indigo Soul is born knowing their purpose. However, the human parent attempts to mold the soul by providing the same experiences as they themselves were raised with. The challenge is that these Indigo Souls were not meant to "be" what this world considers "typical." These souls more than likely do not desire to be a lawyer, accountant, or mechanic. They probably were those things (and more) in previous lifetimes!

The parent of today is ill-prepared to raise the Indigo Soul of tomorrow, because you try and try again to make them something they are not...you.

An Indigo will rebel and refuse to move forward with their purpose if they feel that their own intuition is wrong. If they do not feel safe, if they do not feel accepted to do what to them is natural, then they won't. They will just STOP. As a guardian, think of yourself as a bodyguard. Of course you must protect a child from physical dangers. More so, you must block the judgments, questioning, and attempts to rationalize. Why does this child not act like all the others? Why does this child's behavior not conform? As the bodyguard you must deflect the negativity that is directed towards this soul. Protect it from sensing, feeling, receiving negative energy that may thwart them from moving forward.

**Indigo is not a label to explain away behavior.
Indigo is a purpose.**

Every soul has to experience at least one human lifetime. Souls that have already fulfilled that requirement, many times over, were purposely chosen to come again as Indigo. The natural evolution of the human race has caused destruction to planet Earth and all of God's creatures. Destruction, of many shapes and sizes, has seeped into everything, impacting everything. Although modern medicine is a wonderful discovery, and technological advances are wonderful invention, visible and invisible damage is a result of such progress.

Regardless of your spiritual beliefs, there is no misunderstanding that miracles through faith happen every day. From where do these exceptional happenings transpire? Source! If the human race can accept that Source energy can heal, and there are souls, right now, on this Earth that can transmit energy at the vibration required, why isn't it being done? Why isn't this energy leveraged to heal that which is suffering?

The Indigo Soul is meant to heal through Source energy.

Illness, any illness, can be healed through Source. Indigo Souls are meant to transmit Source. Actually, any person can be schooled in the art of healing to transmit Source. However, an Indigo, though they look the same on the outside, and they look the same on the inside, they are not the same. An Indigo's energy: surrounding them, living in them, *it is them*, can transmit a higher energy wave pattern for a longer period of time. It is really quite simple. What mankind has been missing is the conduit that is specifically made for the energy you seek.

The Indigo is a specially made conduit for Source energy.

Think of electricity flowing through a wire. If too much electricity is surged through a wire that was not meant to hold that amount, the wire may short circuit. Yet, if the wire was intended to allow an unlimited quantity of electrical current, the energy will continue to flow with little to no resistance.

Any soul can be educated to flow Source energy (think of healing with white light). However, an Indigo Soul's **purpose** is to *radiate Source Energy.* Indigo refers to the essence of their energy. And yes, it's blue light.

The planet has been moving toward crisis for years. God sent Indigo Scouts. The intent was for these souls to find their way to purpose with little to no guidance; after all, they had been here before! With parents and guardians that were unprepared to understand anything about their child, left to their own devices, most of these souls (unfortunately) conformed to society and were unable to find their way. Some did create a path that was a hybrid of a traditional career with their true purpose as a healer; some, but not enough. The next wave of Indigo Souls did not come alone; there were preceded by souls with a Navigator Archetype. Arnette is the Navigator Soul to Jacob, the Indigo Soul.

A Navigator does not read a map, a Navigator makes the map.

It took 40 years in the making for Arnette to take action. It took 5 more years dedicated to personal awareness and growth. It took 4 more years to "hear and understand." As a direct result of this Navigator's experiences, we now have a **YOUNG** Indigo Soul skilled in the healing art of Reiki! Instead of struggling for years with the risk of self-destructive behavior, feeling lost or confused, or simply unfulfilled, we have an Indigo Soul committed to their purpose for the next 60, 70 or maybe even 80 human years!!

Though the soul in your care may indeed have certain characteristics that make it difficult to function in today's society, do you feel that the soul in your care is a healer? Possibly in the traditional sense like a doctor or nurse, but we are talking about careers that do not currently exist today. These souls are here to help this world. It will take courage, not theirs, yours. There are many Earth Angels that you can have ask on your behalf. "Is my child an Indigo?" Unfortunately, there are people that would tell you yes, even though the answer is actually no. As we know the answer will be true, seek out the GoIndigo™ team, as we are who brought them together. We know this to be their truth.

PREPARE TO NAVIGATE

If you are still reading our words you either have suspicion, or validation, that your child is an Indigo Soul. Congratulations! Not because your child is an Indigo Soul, but rather YOU have put forth effort into figuring out why your child is the way that he/she is versus just burying your head in the sand or throwing up your hands and leaving it be! That is the first step of fulfilling your purpose as a Navigator (Parent or Guardian = Navigator). Now that you know, you can exercise free will to accept the journey ahead, or, decline and allow this Indigo Soul to find their path without any guidance. We shall assume the former, and we welcome you!

Allow your souls to speak to each other and remind each other of the agreement you made long before this lifetime:

Embrace the uniqueness
Encourage the exceptions
Conform to nothing
Agree to continue
The questions will come
The answers are here

How can I prepare? What should I do?

Relax. Know that "traditional" does not apply and that is all right. Since educational systems are geared toward reading, writing and arithmetic, taught in an enclosed classroom for X number of hours, for X number of days; realize your Indigo child will last as long as they can, until they just...can't. You will be very fortunate indeed if your child is successful in school through to completion; more than fortunate if they continue on through a college or university. Do not judge yourself on the successes or failures of your child. Be courageous enough to not be affected by what the general population may think. It is a difficult road for the guardian. It is even a more difficult road for the Indigo without you by their side.

An Indigo Soul is amazingly blessed if their Navigator soul is also a natural healer. We must admit this is an anomaly. Most Indigos are paired with a left brained "logical" thinker, which can be an advantage, but also a disadvantage. The logical thinker has to fight their nature, open their mind to the possibility of the intangible and embrace their own ability to be a healer (as you ALL have the ability to be). It is important to practice work/life balance in your own life and lead by example. Read on.

OWN YOUR WELLNESS

Walk, outside. Nature is good for the soul. Find a walking trail versus a sidewalk or road. **Hike.** It's another excellent preferred activity. This is something your souls will enjoy doing together. Any activity that is engaging Mother Earth will provide both mental and physical rewards. **Swim,** outside. Not in a pool of hardened concrete and chemicals. Find a stream, lake, or ocean, as water is soothing to the body. This brings relaxation to the mind and peace to the soul. Begin the practice of **Yoga.** No one form of yoga is better than another. Any participation will provide you with a foundation. We strongly recommend Yoga as an activity for your Indigo as soon as possible, more so than traditional sports that are competitive in nature. Introduce **meditation** into your routine. Meditation is to intentionally put forth effort to train the mind into a relaxed state of consciousness. Some people prefer guided meditation; where a teacher walks you through steps of visualization. Others prefer listening to soft music or the sounds of nature. Begin with 5 to 15 minutes a day. Gradually work up to no time constraints and find that meditation can last for as long as it is meant to! Your initial reaction may be "that is unacceptable. I do not have that kind of time." Finding time is a choice. Be open and honest about what you are doing. The natural curiosity of the child will be awakened.

If you have a passion for fishing and want to share that experience with your child, YOU teach them. If the family recipe for baking is a secret, YOU teach them. The topics we have discussed thus far are not freely discussed in traditional education systems. Physical education focuses on traditional sports such as football, basketball, and volleyball. Not yoga. Students will run around a track, not hike in the woods. Quiet time is for taking a test or watching a movie; never for meditation. With these activities: walking, hiking, swimming, yoga and meditation we exude positive energy. You may find that your Indigo may not voluntarily do these activities alone, but are more than willing to do them with you. Take this opportunity to set an example for the Indigo Soul that this self direct commitment is important. If they do not learn the benefit from you, where will they learn it?

**The vibrations are resonating and your souls
begin to remember why you are here.**

TEAM BUILDING

Being part of a team is an amazing synergy. Unfortunately, most people do not utilize the most powerful team available; that of their own Angels and Spirit Guides. Each and every human soul was accompanied to Earth with Angels provide by their God (for you and you alone). An Angel from God has never experienced a human existence. They are as fascinated by you as you are of them. Angels live with you, through you, *for you*. However, God provided very specific guidelines in that an Angel can in no way influence your free will, the ability to have choice; unless asked by you, they cannot intercede.

Think of it like a sporting event where your family, friends and Angels are all sitting in the bleachers of a gymnasium cheering you on to victory. You fall, and for whatever reason, you cannot get back up. They all sit paralyzed in the stands watching. They so want to come down to join you, to help you, in any way that they can. Your Angels sit there as well, encouraging you to *ask: simply ask*. One simple thought "please help me" provides them the permission to swoop in and surround you with love, support and energy. Angels are not to be called only for when misfortune happens, quite the opposite! Invite your Angels everywhere! Ask them to surround you in white light to keep you safe on a journey. Ask them to help you know, what you need to know, when you need to know it. Bask in their glory and allow them to fulfill *their* true purpose: to walk along side you, as part of you, and experience this life, *together*.

Arnette has an interesting relationship with her Angels. When she needs them (really needs them) she taps a flat surface and says "Tap in, Angels, tap in." We do not understand her humor but her friends do.

You may also be blessed with a family member or friend that has left this life time and returned home to Source. They too may provide guidance in a time of need and are lovingly referred to as Guardian Angels. Jacob has two; an uncle who passed when Jacob was ten and a great grandfather whom he never personally met. There are Earth Angels that are gifted in communicating with these souls as well. Interestingly enough, Angels like to give you tangible proof of their existence: loose feathers, found coins, or light bulbs constantly going out in your presence. Allow yourself to acknowledge them. It will benefit you both.

Spirit Guides are also a part of your team. Unlike Angels, they have had human lifetimes, many human lifetimes, and seek to help you find enlightenment. Experience happiness with your **Joy Guide**. Feel safe and secure with your **Protector**. Know you are cared for by your **Alchemist**. And aspire for personal growth through your **Teacher**. Many societies do not openly welcome discussions about what cannot be seen nor heard. However, we have asked Arnette to share her experience specific to this topic in hopes that you too will be open and allow your own Spirit Guides to reveal themselves to you.

I'm fortunate here in Austin to have access to gifted Earth Angels that have provided such amazing experiences to me. One woman, whom I found through mutual friends, is blessed with the ability to communicate with Spirit Guides and will provide an introduction. "Sometimes" she explained, "it's easier to have a conversation and reach out for help from someone who has a face and a name."

I was so pleased to have met my Joy Guide "Prissy" who wondered why we had stopped painting. I found such peace and happiness painting at my kitchen table. I do have some talent. I've matted and framed paintings and they hang in my home. Prissy said "you stopped Arnette because you believe that every piece has to be perfect, every piece needs to be displayed. You put so much pressure on yourself that you lost the joy." She was right. Prissy also enjoys roller coasters as well, which really works to my advantage!

Leopold is an extremely large Viking-ish Warrior with a long red beard, massive arms and a fairly large belly (though it doesn't slow him down one bit). He is strong as an ox and as gentle as a bunny. He pokes fun at how uptight I am and is always trying to get me to relax. No harm will come to me. He always has my back (so he exclaims while taking a bite out of a bird leg). I know he is with me. One time, I found myself in a situation where I could not move (literally, acupuncture tends to keep you immobile). I was scared by some strange anomalies that made them known through unexplainable noises. "Please make is stop, Leopold. Whatever is happening is really freaking me out." It stopped. Whatever it was, it stopped. (I have a witness).

I must admit I do not call on Dr. Frank Barnhardt, my Alchemist, as frequently as I should. Especially when I'm feeling under the weather. Even I forget what is available to me in my own tool chest of resources.

When it was time for me to meet my Teacher, he refused to partake. He refused to be introduced to me. He said "We have met before. I am insulted she does not recall. She must remember on her own if she is to learn anything." I was embarrassed in front of this woman who was facilitating this session with my guides. But I was also hurt. I am trying to learn. I am trying to grow. I was filled with self doubt. After all this, I'm not good enough to meet my own Teacher?

That night I sat with my pendulum and attempted to relax my mind and allow myself to remember. I asked for guidance to take me back to that point in time where I had met my Teacher. By God, I did.

I had a "dream" a few years ago. My dreams are like movies in living color. I was with my parents in the middle of a desert standing in a circular enclosure. It was surrounded by caves stacked two stories high. Each cave had a very beautiful arched wooden door with ornate carvings around it. Many people were milling around... waiting. But I didn't know what we were waiting for. I glanced up to a second story cave with a window. I could see the flicker of a light, like the room was dark but there was a television on. I saw the shadow of someone walking by that window. Suddenly, the crowd stilled and then hushed tones said "he's coming, he's finally coming out." The crowd parted to allow this amazing **Being** to walk through. He was wearing the most vibrant red feathered headdress and wore a long red robe with gold trimming. He was so tall and broad chested. He was regal. He was important, and he was walking right toward me. I quickly looked at my parents, yet I was frozen in place. The word "shaman" was what I heard. He gently put his hand on my head and smoothed it down, gathering my long hair and pulling it over my shoulder. He took my right hand, palm up and drew a red X with his finger. He had me kneel down in a child's pose (I knew that from yoga). He then took two fingers and placed them at the bottom of my skull and traced his fingers down my spine.

Then I woke up.

It was no dream. I was at my own blessing ceremony. I do know that man. He's my Teacher. He's my Chief.

Months later (after this realization) I was at my first ever acupuncture appointment. While I'm lying on the table, the Dr. of Oriental Medicine said to me (this is our first meeting) "Um, do you happen to know a really large imposing man dressed all in red?" I said simply, yet confidently, "Yes, I do. That's my Chief." She chuckled and said, "Well, just so you know, he showed up here before you did and wants to know what the heck I'm planning on doing to you today because there's nothing wrong with you." Chief continues to show up to all my appointments before me; keeping quiet, yet always watching.

How many children have imaginary friends with parents who are "uncomfortable" with how much time is spent alone, playing with "those friends." Are you one of those parents? Both you and the Indigo Soul in your care have Angels and Spirit Guides waiting to help you on your journey. When Arnette shared this story with Jacob, he said "I know my protector. He's Hawaiian and wears turquoise blue with blue stripes painted on his face. I met him in my dreams. I call him My Blue Man." Jacob was proud to say it. He knows a trip to Hawaii is in his plans someday, to walk the same ground as this powerful warrior. Speak openly to allow these wonderful interactions to unfold. How commonplace it should be to say, "It is cold outside! Did you remember your jacket? Do not forget to invite your team!"

Acknowledge that you are not alone and forever will you feel their embrace.

CHAKRAS: YOURS AND THEIRS

The body has seven (7) main energy centers called Chakras. You may be introduced to them while participating in Yoga. The chakras must be kept "moving" to live a life of allowing. If a chakra is sluggish your own energy cannot flow freely. If a chakra is sluggish Source energy cannot flow freely. Blockages can cause physical or emotional distress. Both the healer and the recipient must have open chakras for the exchange of energy to flow. A healer should confirm all chakras are moving energy or be prepared to clear them (see Image 1). As a Navigator it will be advantageous for you to know, as well.

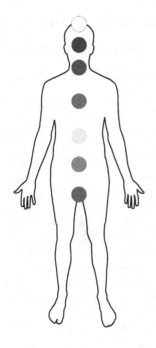

7th (white): *The Crown Chakra represents our ability to be fully connected spiritually.*

6th (purple): *The Third Eye Chakra represents our ability to focus and see the big picture.*

5th (blue): *The Throat Chakra represents our ability to communicate.*

4th (green): *The Heart Chakra represents our ability to love.*

3rd (yellow): *The solar Plexus Chakra represents our ability to be confident and in-control of our lives.*

2nd (orange): *The Sacral Chakra represents our ability to accept others and new experiences.*

1st (red): *The Root Chakra represents our foundation and being grounded.*

How do I know if chakras are moving freely? ASK

The most practical way to ask if a chakra is flowing energy freely or is sluggish is by using a **pendulum.** A pendulum is simply a tool used to receive a yes or no answer to a question. The pendulum is able to swing based on the energy that surrounds it. The direction of the pendulum swing dictates the answer. The pendulum is a natural extension of an individual skilled in the art of healing. Similar to how a stethoscope is a tool for a physician.

Pendulums come in a variety of shapes and sizes, from very simple to very ornate. They can be representative of the healer that uses it. Arnette explained the pendulum to her Indigo children with this analogy,  "Remember when Harry Potter went to purchase his very first wand? The owner of Ollivanders Wand[13] shop explained that you don't choose the wand, the wand chooses you." Selecting your first pendulum is a similar experience. Look for a pendulum you find pleasing. Hold it as instructed and say "Show me movement." If you have been practicing meditation and yoga, your vibration may be high enough to receive a swing. This is your pendulum! If there is no movement, try another. Do not be disappointed if you receive no movement. Simply select the pendulum that speaks to you the most.

---

[13]   Ollivanders Wand Shop, Harry Potter Book Series by J.K. Rowlings, Harper Collins Publishing.

A pendulum must be *cleared* and *programmed* before it will respond correctly. Always begin with a prayer of protection.

Holy Creator (God, Allah, etc.)
Please surround me in white light and protect me
as I ask my Spirit Guides and Angels
to help me in using this tool
as a way to communicate with the energies around and for me
always on behalf of my highest self, never ego.

Arnette's pendulum swings clockwise for a "yes" and it swings north and south (vs. east/west) for a "no." Pendulums do respond differently though it can be programmed to respond in the way which is more comfortable to you. Ask the store personnel to assist you, they can be most helpful. Some individuals are more vibrationally inclined to move any pendulum they pick up. Do not despair if it takes awhile; practice makes perfect. Most likely, a pendulum will swing immediately for your Indigo the very first time! Asking questions of a pendulum cannot tell the future. It is a tool to assist "right here, right now" which is all that matters anyway.

Using the pendulum to verify all chakra energies are flowing is an easy exercise. Simply hold the pendulum in front of the root chakra and wait to receive the confirmation of yes. Move to the Sacral Chakra and so on through to the Crown Chakra. If the pendulum swings "no", direct it to flow more easily (as if to open up) until it shows as "yes"... and it will! *(Please note this may be an over simplification in some instances and may require assistance from a more practiced healer).* Why is this important? It is important for you to be wide open (allowing), and for the Indigo as well. Growing up Indigo has its own trials and tribulations. (For anyone) Any negative emotion could cause sluggish chakras. Help your Indigo to have free flowing energy at all times. If your child is having difficulty transitioning to a new city or school, double check their Root Chakra. If your child is fearful or nervous in giving an oral presentation, double check their Throat Chakra. If your child has loved and lost a pet, friend or relative, double check their Heart Chakra.

**With a free flowing Chakra the benefits
are endless, the lesson is timeless.**

BODYGUARD 101

The ability to protect the Indigo Soul is most important. Previously we discussed the concept of "bodyguard." We do not refer to the obvious: food, clothing, and shelter, or even safety from physical dangers. We are already aware that negative emotions such as judgment, ridicule, fear, ignorance are all harmful if directed toward any soul, yet especially painful to the Indigo. Now we are referring to another danger, an unseen danger. Harmful to you, but especially harmful to Indigo: Negative Entities.

**Do not just understand the personality
of your child: <u>know it</u>.**

Pay attention to changes in moods, temperament, and attitude. Many times you assume behavioral changes are due to being overly tired, hormones, or the all encompassing teenage angst. When out in public you may be apologetic on behalf of your child's behavior but then in private will scold and punish them.

Spirits are souls that did not cross over. They did not follow the light when it was their time. Possibly because they were afraid, or had unfinished business, or just delayed a moment too long and lost the opportunity. They will wander, looking for the light. Spirits are attracted to your energy, but especially Indigo energy because their essence is "light." They will not harm your child, but they might speak to them! Whereas, a Negative Entity is spirit that also did not cross over; probably on purpose, probably for malicious intent. They did not want to leave. They will avoid leaving. However, they need the energy of a physical body. Therefore, they attach to animals or people. This can disrupt a person's behavior. Negative Entities are especially drawn to the essence/light of an Indigo Soul. The more you evolve in your own personal growth the more open you are to an attachment as well.

Everyone has an energy field that other people step in or through. The more people you encounter, the higher the risk. Think of the areas where you are exposed to crowds: the airport, a movie theater, a shopping mall, even school. If you are emotionally vulnerable, weak due to illness, the more susceptible the body becomes. As a bodyguard you need to protect yourself, your dwelling, and most importantly, the Indigo in your care.

How do I know if Negative Entities are present? Ask

Do not be afraid. Prior to any attempt at communication always protect yourself. The action of "asking" is raising your vibration, which in turn attracts both good and bad energies. Therefore, hold your pendulum and begin with prayer. This is merely a simple and easy example to remember, but there is no right or wrong:

Who	Say	Action
Navigator	Holy Creator (God, Allah, etc.) Please surround me with your white light and protect me as I ask for guidance from my Spirit Guides and Angels at this time. Always on behalf of my highest self, never ego.	Your pendulum should begin to swing "yes" as the white light, Guides and Angels come in, then ask it to stop.
Navigator	May I please ask for assistance from (say child's name) Spirit Guides and Angels at this time Always on behalf of his/her highest self, never ego.	Your pendulum should begin to swing "yes" again as they come in, then ask it to stop.
Option 1	Depending on where you are (if inside, open a window or door) you can firmly tell them to leave. It was not invited here. It cannot stay. Continue to force the issue until your pendulum confirms it is gone. Unfortunately, it will just find another energy source to attach to.	Pendulum should begin to swing "no."
Option 2	Ask an Archangel for assistance. Call in Archangel Michael or Raphael to assist in removing this negative entity from your child. Ask to surround it in white light. Explain this entity was not invited here and it cannot stay. Request the Angel escort the entity from the premises. Always thank the Angel. Wave your arm up and down around your child to cut any invisible chords of energy.	Pendulum should begin to swing "no."

Remember previously Arnette being angry with Jacob and frustrated many times over unacceptable behavior? Taking away electronic devices or driving privileges were met with indifference and "I don't care" responses. Now it is second nature to use a pendulum to check for possible reasons as to why. She's looking for Entities. Realize that as your skills and vibrations increase, it is like having a spotlight on your house, drawing more attention than you realize. Once an Indigo's vibrations begin to mature, your home becomes even more of a beacon for uninvited guests. It will continue to be a constant battle to keep your space and your loved ones "clear." Be diligent in establishing a routine: pay attention to what is, but more importantly, what is "not normal" behavior for the people living in your home. If you validate a presence, clear it.

As you become more confident we encourage you to seek guidance from more skilled teachers to truly understand your options with protection and Negative Entities (and other uninvited visitors).

REIKI FOR...EVERYONE!

Reiki is the universal art of natural healing that positively affects the whole person including the body, emotions, mind and spirit. The word Reiki means "universal life force energy." The Indigo Soul will grow into their role as a healer, but you must understand what that means. YOU can be a healer now. Every person on planet Earth has the aptitude and the ability to learn this ancient art form. This does not mean that all Navigators are intended to stop working in their current profession and begin a Reiki practice (but you could if that is your desire).

- With Reiki I, the student (you and your Indigo) receive the Reiki first degree attunement, guided to great healing power. You learn the history and the art of Reiki healing and how to facilitate full body treatments on yourself and others.
- With Reiki II, the student (you and your Indigo) receive the Reiki second degree attunement to further increase the healing power. You gain conscious knowledge of

the sounds and symbols and their application in body treatments, emotional healing, and in daily life.

- With Advanced Reiki, the student (the Indigo) receives the Reiki master attunement to increase the strength of the healing power. They will learn advanced techniques to solve problems and achieve goals.

- As a Master, the student receives the Reiki master/ teacher attunement, moving further along a path of personal self-mastery and gaining the ability to pass on the power and understanding of Reiki to others.

As a Navigator, it is recommended that you earn your Reiki I & II degrees so you may provide emotional and physical healing to others; even if it is only for immediate family and friends, or the family pets. Watching you, hearing you, will resonate with the Indigo providing exposure in a safe, non threatening way. The Indigo Soul will think, "If my parent or guardian believes in the power of Reiki, and accepts it as being a normal part of our daily life, then it is okay!"

The immune system is constantly under attack. People visit a doctor at the first sign of a sniffle. Animals are taken to a veterinarian for vaccines. Alternative medicine or natural remedies are the exception not the norm; usually not even pursued as a viable option until traditional medicinal avenues have been exhausted. Wouldn't it be nice if more people were aware of, and understood, the power of Reiki? Wouldn't it be nice if Reiki was the chosen path to wellness for both humans and animals alike?

Wouldn't it be nice if Reiki intervention helped to escalate natural disaster recovery? The Indigo Soul has the ability to be instrumental in this and more; if given the opportunity.

Allow your Indigo children to "be" children until their Indigo Soul matures and reaches for its purpose. We must raise them with a strong foundation (yoga, meditation) and provide opportunity to engage and study with a Reiki Master at the starting point of their journey to purpose. Our intent is for every Indigo Soul to be a Reiki Master (and more).

This is the mindset that must be taught and it begins with you, Navigator.

EDUCATION: INDIGO STYLE

We understand education is one of the most difficult aspects of raising the Indigo Soul. The Indigo Scouts, if they have a successful academic career, more than likely they achieved it through sheer determination and fortitude. Indigo Souls are intelligent and creative individuals. Unfortunately, their gifts usually are suppressed in traditional classrooms.

Think back to when you were a child. A hurtful word or a pitying look wounded your pride (ego). A hurtful word or a pitying look directed toward an Indigo, wounds the soul (highest self) as they can truly "feel the negativity of the action." It is not that the Indigo is incapable of achieve academic successes; far from it! Unfortunately, the environment of most educational institutions is not conducive to their comfort (their emotional and physical well-being) which in turn inhibits learning. Add to that a common trait of an Indigo: being stubborn. Another common trait of an Indigo: inability to conform. And we wonder why an Indigo child struggles.

In school, a child between the ages of 5-10 is usually with the same children all day every day. They can learn and manage the energy of 30 other children (along with their Angels and Spirit Guides.) In the United States public school system, from ages 11-13 the Indigo may now be managing the energy of approximately 210 different (7 classes * 30) students along with their Angels and Spirit Guides as well! The constant transferring to classes mean the Indigo Soul's energy field is crossed numerous times. It is like ripping a band-aid off exposing their vibration. With all this "invisible activity" going on around them, they are expected to be alert, focused and engaged. It can become overwhelming. Unfortunately, they do not know why they feel the way they do; let alone trying to explain it. Frustration is the leading cause of acting out. Acting out is disruptive, disruption is frowned upon. A never ending cycle ensues. Or as in Jacob's case, he just "mentally checked out" versus being a bother or inconvenience to anyone.

The early (school) years are meant for awareness, socialization, communication, creativity, friendship, laughter, play and love. An Indigo Soul does need education: how to tell time, how to handle money, how to navigate transportation systems. They need basic survival skills to function in today's world.

Realize that academics (in the grand scheme of things) may be a very small blip on a very big screen.

Since Indigos are notoriously stubborn, maybe yours will succeed in a traditional educational system just to prove they can. In the early grades, we prefer the Montessori School model, or finding a school environment that is supportive of collaborative learning which allows movement and creative exchange. Or, possibly consider home schooling. If none of these are viable options, follow Arnette's lead and take the "social norm" regarding academics out of the equation. Do not fight the system, just flow with it until there is no longer a need to. A high school diploma and entrance exams required as acceptance into universities are not applicable here. Their path toward healing with not be found within those walls.

An Indigo Soul has such a strong sense of self they cannot easily modify their behavior to make other people comfortable. Accept me as I am. If you cannot, so be it.

By the time your Indigo reaches the age of 15-17 the ability to just "go along with the normal expectations" is in direct conflict with everything they fundamentally "are." The internal struggle begins, so they withdraw. They seek quiet because there is a constant "internal noise" which they assume to be remnants from too much socialization (school), but it is not. Noise is from spirit attempting to gain their attention. Headaches or migraines are also a sign of spirit trying to make contact. Indigo try and stop the internal noise with external noise: listening to music, watching television or partaking in video games. This is merely an escape mechanism. Do not take it personally as if you have done something wrong. An Indigo Soul is inclined toward an addictive personality and may choose drugs or alcohol to stop noise as well. (This is also why an early introduction to yoga and meditation may redirect them from even attempting to go down this path.) Always on their mind is "Why do I feel this way? Why am I not like the others? Why am I not motivated to do what they do, to be as they are?" Do not allow them to withdraw from YOU (gently). It is time to speak with them about what "being Indigo" truly means.

> *"God brought you here for a very special reason. With Reiki, you have the ability to heal that which is broken; the planet, the animals, people. God identifies you as "Indigo." Together, we will pursue what this specifically means for YOU but to understand the purpose of all Indigo is the same: to heal. I have been preparing for this day. I am your Navigator."*

Allow them time to acknowledge this declaration, process it, and know they may choose otherwise. Our hope is they will acknowledge it as their truth. Now the journey to purpose truly begins.

THE PATTERN

Reflect on the events that bring the most joy to your Indigo.

Are they always outside? Digging in the sandbox or playing in the dirt? From sun up until sun down, is your child always in the woods, at the park, in the lake, at the beach, fishing in the river, floating down a stream, laying in a hammock, napping in the shade, sitting by the campfire? Their affinity is for the **Earth.**

Are they always bringing home stray animals? Are they always watching animal shows on the television? Is their bed where all the family pets sleep? Would they notice if an animal was hurt and want you to stop the vehicle? Is their favorite vacation to the zoo, but they want the animals free? Their affinity is for **animals.**

Do all the infants and toddlers love your child? Does your child have an exceptionally close relationship with a grandparent? Does your child want to make sandwiches for the homeless? Does your child speak out on behalf of other children they feel have been wronged? Does your child have strong opinions about war or transgressions against other people? Does your child get lost in history or learning about new cultures? Their affinity is for **people**.

Indigo Souls, along with the power of Reiki, can direct their healing toward anything. To focus energy for what they have a natural affinity for is an unstoppable combination. Remember this is unchartered territory. There is no guidebook on choosing a career path. How will my Indigo child be able to make a living? Do not focus on the "how" only focus on the "what." What will they do? What do they want to do is the more appropriate question. There are no limitations!

Do not fear the unknown as that same fear will only limit the wants from becoming known.

You have the tools to lay the groundwork which in turn set the wheels in motion. Allow the universe to provide rest.

Blessed is the soul of the Indigo

~Abraham

ARNETTE: READY, SET, GO INDIGO

Indigo and Crystal Children

Archangel Metatron: "You have a bond with children. In particular, you can help children who are sensitive."

Teaching and Learning

Archangel Zadkiel: "Keep an open mind, and learn new ideas. Then, teach these ideas to others."

Creative Writing

Archangel Gabriel: "Make time to write down your thoughts in a journal, or pen an article or book."

For the past few years I receive the same three Angel Cards[14]. If not all three displaying in the same session, any combination of two was inevitable. The Indigo and Crystal Children card was, and continues to be, no surprise.

By formal education, I am a High School teacher. By profession, I implement software for Learning & Development

---

[14] Doreen Virtue PhD. Guidebook for Archangel Oracle Cards, (Hay House Publishing 2004).

organizations at the corporate level. I am often in front of an audience discussing a company's strategy and the infrastructure to support that strategy (blah, blah, blah). In my narrowed mind I assumed the Teaching and Learning card made reference to this (it made sense to me). And lastly, I write in a journal all the time. To me, a diary would capture what I've done, where I've been. A journal contains what I want for myself and my children. It reflects my inner most thoughts, hopes and dreams (my wants). So I thought I was covered in regards to the Creative Writing card as well. What I now understand is that these cards were messages from my Angels letting me know of the changes that were coming (for me). Abraham is my messenger now.

In March of 2013 when I realized Jake would need assistance with most things in regards to running his own business, Abraham had asked me, *"What about the other Indigo, Arnette? What about them?"* I quickly realized that reaching out to the Navigator population was just the beginning. The intention of Abraham was always to guide me in creating the infrastructure to provide on-going education for Indigo Souls and to create job opportunities where none have ever existed before. We have been blessed by many Earth Angels long before me who have worked diligently to break down the barriers to holistic healing. They have done a tremendous job at keeping many types of practices alive and available to those who seek them out. Thank you all! We hope to apprentice many Indigo healers with the amazingly gifted traditional healers spread worldwide.

You may ask, "Why now?" Because now we have the older Indigo Scouts available with the life skills, they just need to learn how to access their gifts. We have younger Indigo Souls, like Jacob, who are ready to learn their craft yet need to gain necessary life skills. And finally, we have an entire population of Indigo Souls still "in school" and are depending on us to have all the "red tape" worked out and running smoothly by the time they are ready to take the next step.

An Indigo Soul will surpass their teacher; it can be no other way.

This is a very profound statement. I must admit, my ego was a little bruised. This was quickly erased when I realized that God never meant for me to be a healing practitioner. God did, however, mean for me to bridge both worlds. Although an Indigo Soul does not normally have the personality or probably the desire to pave a way through traditional society; I do. Abraham has assembled GoIndigo™ with a highly qualified team of Indigo aware resources that have the strategic vision to make this a reality. For key teaching positions we've coordinated Indigo Scout resources that magically appeared in my life over the last few years. The GoIndigo™ Non-Profit Organization has curriculum designed specifically for Navigators to support and prepare for the transition. The Indigo Soul curriculum uses learning modalities geared toward learning Indigo Style (which traditional higher-education and trade schools will never provide). We focus specifically on content Abraham has deemed necessary to prepare an Indigo Soul in leading a life of purpose in some type of healing capacity.

We've drafted three Affinity Charts: Animal, People and Earth. Every Indigo has a natural affinity (probably more than one). Navigate the four branches (for each affinity) to see what their specific interest might be. Once they've reached maturity[15] which is unique per Indigo (could be as early as 16 or into their 20's) these affinity branches are possible areas where we (GoIndigo™) can help facilitate their journey to purpose. As they reach their vibrational peak, additional gifts will begin to surface ranging anywhere from animal communication to assisting souls cross over. This is where key partnerships with specialized Light Workers will be more necessary than ever. We are all responsible for creating a safe environment for them to do their work. We must all embrace their uniqueness, and send thanks for sending them to us.

If the information in this book speaks to your soul in any way, please visit our website at www.goindigohealing.com for more information about GoIndigo™ Non-Profit Organization education and professional services. And the child on his *journey to purpose*, the one who started it all? Jacob has transitioned from being a vet tech to boarding & kennel services (which include providing Reiki). He is also an Animal

---

[15] Maturity refers to completion of an academic program (i.e. high school diploma, GED) where the Indigo is legally able to pursue ongoing education and begin to earn taxable wages.

Affinity Team Lead at GoIndigo™. Within the walls of the (soon to be) GoIndigo™ Stables & Kennels he plans to establish a Senior Dog Sanctuary.

We look forward to greeting you at our open door.

Buckle up!

~Arnette, Master Navigator

INDIGO AFFINTY
CHART – ANIMALS

WORKING/SERVICE

Military/Police Canine
Police/Healing Horses
Search & Rescue
Show (Equestrian, race, etc.)

DOMESTIC

Home
Farm
Shelter

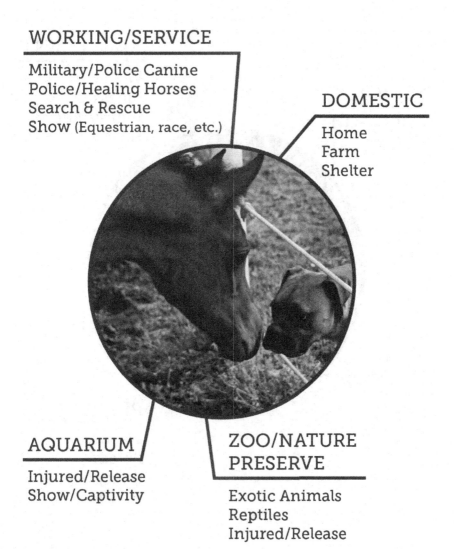

AQUARIUM

Injured/Release
Show/Captivity

ZOO/NATURE PRESERVE

Exotic Animals
Reptiles
Injured/Release

INDIGO AFFINITY
CHART – PEOPLE

ADOLECENT

Wellness
Illness
Injury/Illness
Hospice

SENIOR

Assisted Living
Hospice

ADULT

Wellness
Illness
Injury/Illness
Hospice

PEDIATRIC

Wellness
Illness
Injury/Illness
Hospice

INDIGO AFFINITY
CHART – EARTH

AGRICULTURE

Farm/Crops
Orchard
Forest Restoration
Natural Resources

INDUSTRIAL POLLUTION

Air
Toxic Spills

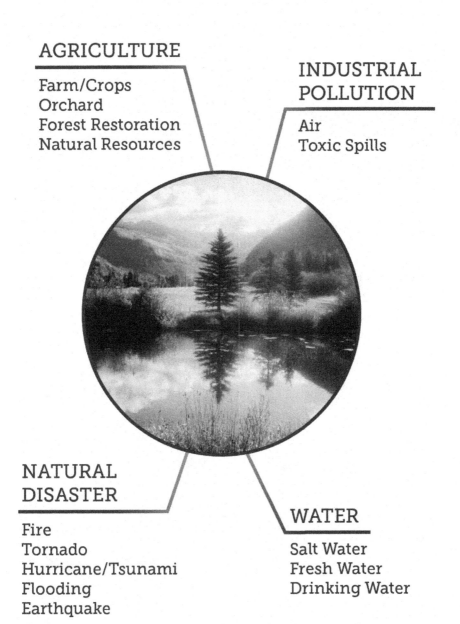

NATURAL DISASTER

Fire
Tornado
Hurricane/Tsunami
Flooding
Earthquake

WATER

Salt Water
Fresh Water
Drinking Water

Printed in the United States
By Bookmasters